By George!... is a must read since all of us are CEOs of our own lives! Leadership is always critical... in good times and during challenging times. Bill D'Arienzo cleverly, clearly, and consistently compares George Washington's lessons of leadership that he demonstrated as America's CEO (General of the Continental Army) with our country's business CEO leaders. We who believe in the greatness of our country and the power and importance of leadership, will gain a lot by following the lessons suggested by Bill D'Arienzo in *By George*...

—Jack Mitchell, CEO of Mitchells/ Richards / Marshs and author of *Hug Your Customer* (Hyperion 2003) and *Hug Your People* (Hyperion 2008)

In *By George! Lessons in leadership from George Washington, CEO,* William D'Arienzo gives readers a fresh and insightful look at the Father of His Country through the eyes of a corporate advisor. Written in a crisp and compelling style, this brief book focuses on Washington's character and personnel skills during the Revolution, and derives principles that today's CEO's would do well to apply.

—Jeffry H. Morrison, Associate Professor of Government, Regent University, and author of *The Political Philosophy of George Washington* (Johns Hopkins University Press, 2009)

Treasonous subordinates, unmotivated employees, time-tested and wise opponents, try naming an organizational or leadership challenge Washington didn't face! Yet he overcame every potentially fatal problem in ways that are instructive to all of us, especially CEOs. Most amazingly, Washington's example successfully breaks many common sense rules, and Bill D'Arienzo in *By George!*... presents these insights in a clear and lively narrative. This is learning from the past in the best and most effective way.

—John Agresto, University President and author of *The Liberation of Iraq and the Failure of Good Intentions (*Encounter Books, 2007)

BY GEORGE!

BILL D'ARIENZO, PhD

BY GEORGE!

LESSONS IN LEADERSHIP
FROM GEORGE WASHINGTON, CEO

TATE PUBLISHING & *Enterprises*

By George
Copyright © 2010 by Bill D'Arienzo, PhD. All rights reserved.

This title is also available as a Tate Out Loud product. Visit www.tatepublishing.com for more information.

No part of this publication may be reproduced, stored in a retrieval system or transmitted in any way by any means, electronic, mechanical, photocopy, recording or otherwise without the prior permission of the author except as provided by USA copyright law.

This book is designed to provide accurate and authoritative information with regard to the subject matter covered. This information is given with the understanding that neither the author nor Tate Publishing, LLC is engaged in rendering legal, professional advice.

The opinions expressed by the author are not necessarily those of Tate Publishing, LLC.

Published by Tate Publishing & Enterprises, LLC
127 E. Trade Center Terrace | Mustang, Oklahoma 73064 USA
1.888.361.9473 | www.tatepublishing.com

Tate Publishing is committed to excellence in the publishing industry. The company reflects the philosophy established by the founders, based on Psalm 68:11,
"The Lord gave the word and great was the company of those who published it."

Book design copyright © 2010 by Tate Publishing, LLC. All rights reserved.
Cover design by Tyler Evans
Interior design by Nathan Harmony

Published in the United States of America

ISBN: 978-1-61663-017-1
1. Business & Economics: Leadership
2. Business & Economics: Corporate & Business History
10.02.08

"I think there was never a time, when cool and dispassionate reasoning, strict attention and application, great integrity and...wisdom were more to be wished for..."
—(George Washington to Thomas Nelson, March 15, 1779)

Acknowledgments

Where does one begin? There are too many who have come before me and helped to make the crooked places straight.

My parents who are now passed but still a presence—especially my father, whom I had perhaps longer than a son deserves; affording me a chance to renew what had become tarnished. Kathie DeChirico, who always believed that writing was my destiny and endlessly encouraged me; to my dear friend, scholar and "fratello" Professor Santi V. Buscemi, without whose watchful eye for phrase and syntax, this work would be less than it is; to Katharine Lydon, whose unbridled enthusiasm and patience as my ghost editor was amazing; and to all my professors who taught me to love learning, I acknowledge that this book could not have been written. And to our great country, America, which I truly love, and to the ultimate Source of whatever value this work may have, as nothing comes to be save through the Father—to all I am grateful; what errors there are, are mine; whatever value there is, is the result of all mentioned and unmentioned.

—Written on the 4th of July 2009
Princeton, New Jersey

Table of Contents

13	Preface
17	Introduction
29	The Crucible of Character
37	George Washington Becomes CEO
47	Communicating the Mission Statement
57	Charisma and Paradigm Leadership
65	George Washington as CEO
75	Management by Trust

85	Operations and Delegations
95	Leadership by Example and Crisis Management
105	Conclusion
109	Post Script
111	A Summary of Washington's Leadership Guidelines

Preface

General George Washington headed the Continental Army for eight arduous years. He was instrumental in winning a war against the most powerful navy in the world and the best trained, most disciplined, and well-funded army of its time. He did so despite the fact that many of his troops had no training, shoes, rations, ammunition, or pay. If we consider the entire situation from a business perspective, here is what transpired under Washington's watch as CEO:

- He left a well-established business (his farm) to lead a start-up company (the Continental Army) few thought could succeed.

- He was able to successfully market his product (a nation governed by its own people)

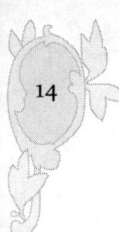

when he had no proprietary product to market and little capital with which to do it.

- His organization had no seasoned executives or trained managers—no one attended business school (i.e., military academy).
- His company had horrendous cash flow problems.
- His company had no core competency.
- He lost an overwhelming number of battles (market share) in which he was engaged, and though he never won a major battle, he remained CEO (Commander in Chief).
- He had no share of the market (territory or countryside) that he could constantly claim as his own.
- He consistently lost the confidence of the Board of Directors (Continental Congress) but was never ousted as CEO.
- He was constantly harassed by his stockholders and stakeholders (citizens and farmers) as to his competence and the strategies he employed to drive the business (the war).

- His own Executive Committee (his General Staff) urged him to declare bankruptcy (surrender), but he refused.

Given all these circumstances, how did the *company* survive and the *business* prosper? Through Washington's leadership! Here's what he did:

- He understood that executive leadership is a *moral responsibility*; it is not primarily for personal gain but a call to serve.
- He did his best from a classical sense of personal honor and professional will.
- When needed, he acted boldly but never impulsively. Yet he had a propensity for action.
- When he was in doubt, without information, he made no premature decisions; he made no decision before its time.
- When overwhelmed by criticism or intransigence from his Board of Directors, he always took the high ground in his arguments to the contrary.
- He never took any criticism of his leadership personally.

- He constantly communicated with integrity, honesty, consistency, and vision with shareholders, stakeholders, and his general staff.
- He led by example—literally and figuratively on the front-lines, leading the charge in the heat of the battle, highly visible to those whom he led.
- He transformed himself into a brand.

Introduction

In the past decade, we witnessed an unprecedented phenomenon in the corporate world. If we were to use a military metaphor it might be described as: *The Relentless Siege and Fall of the CEOs.* The number of short-term leaders of high-profile companies who capitulated to this onslaught is only part of the story. The other part is the ferocity and frequency with which shareholders, stakeholders, and boards of directors summarily sealed their fate.

Both dynamics are unprecedented and underscored by the fact that the economic conditions under which some CEOs operated could not have been better. Increases in sales and profits, large growth in market capitalization, the opening of new world markets and the like, characterized the business milieu. Here is a partial casualty list drawn at random from the littered landscape:

CEO (Year of Demise)	Company	Reason	Tenure / Ended By
Albert Dunlap (1998)	Sunbeam	Poor Performance and Aggressive Style	2 years / Board of Directors
Richard McGinn (2000)	Lucent	Poor Communication and Poor Company Performance	2 years / Board of Directors and Shareholders
Jill Barad (2000)	MATTEL	Poor Performance, Style	2 years / Board of Directors and Investors
Richard Huber (2000)	Aetna	Loss Market Value and Brash Management Style	4 years / Board of Directors and Shareholders
Michael C. Hawley (2000)	Gillette	Company Poor Performance	18 months / Board of Directors

Michael Bonsignore (2001)	Honeywell	Failed Merger and Poor Communication	12 months / Board of Directors
Peter Bijur (2001)	Texaco	Management Style, Arrogant and Poor Company Performance	4 years / Board of Directors and Shareholders
G. Richard Thoman (2001)	XEROX	Communication, Company Lost Faith in Leadership Ability	1 year / Resigned "Under Pressure"
Carl Yankowski (2001)	Majesco Games	Poor Communication, Loss Market Value	12 months / Board of Directors
Carly Fiorina (2005)	Hewlett-Packard	Poor Communication, "Look at Me" Style	6 years / Board of Directors

Robert Nardelli (2006)	Home Depot	Poor, Abrasive Communication	6 years / Board of Directors and Shareholders
Stanley O'Neal (2007)	Merrill Lynch	Lack of Transparency, Poor Communication	4 years / Retired "Under Pressure" from Board of Directors
Jerry Yang (2008)	Yahoo!	Failed Merger and Demeanor/ Style	16 months / Board of Directors and Shareholders
John Thain (2009)	Merrill Lynch	Lack of Transparency, Poor Management Style	13 months / Board of Directors

Conventional wisdom tells us that CEOs are fired (or forced to resign) due to their company's poor financial performance. But according to a recent study from LeadershipIQ.com (confirmed by other sources as well), this commonly-held belief can be readily challenged. Although CEOs are fired because the Board has lost confidence in their ability to meet revenue and profit goals in the near future, it is inevitably a crisis of confidence exasperated by non-fiscal personality, issues of character and/or communication dynamics, which are the catalysts for the decision. Here are the results of the aforementioned study:

- 31 percent of CEOs get fired for mismanaging change
- 28 percent for ignoring customers
- 27 percent for tolerating low performers
- 23 percent for denying reality
- 22 percent for too much talk and not enough action

The research defines "mismanaging change" as: "Failure to motivate and clearly communicate the need to change course." Over 70 percent are reasons of a like kind.

What is clear is that *leadership style*, and most importantly, *communication strategy*, are as important as determinants in a CEO's longevity as is financial performance. Reference the CEO chart listed earlier. Poor communication, abrasive styles, and image issues are cited as major contributors to the downfall of many if not all of these once prominent leaders!

In the 2008 annual survey published by *Booz & Company*, "CEO Succession 2008: Stability in the Storm," "127 CEOs were forced out (the board dismissed the CEO for poor financial performance, an ethical lapse, or irreconcilable differences)" as compared to the 106 CEOs who were forced out just the year before. That is an increase of 17 percent! And the average tenure of a CEO dropped from nine years in 1999 to eight years in 2006, and to 6.7 years in 2008! Ethical lapse (character issues) and irreconcilable differences (communication/leadership style issues) are the prevailing reasons given for dismissal.

So why have the messiahs of modern management answered the call but so often been unable to sustain the faith of their followers? Is the explanation of this

By George!

crisis in leadership to be found in the person's character, his/her performance capabilities, or the paradigm by which he/she leads? An article in *Worth* (May 2001) provides a point of departure:

> A New Kind of business visionary...has made it into the American pantheon—CEOs described as visionary, messianic, missionary...Vision, even when it involves a perfectly accurate understanding of the future, by itself never ensures business success...[without] crucial values [such] as deliberateness and restraint [and] organizational coherence.

However, these leadership qualities may be necessary but are not sufficient to ensure a CEO's success (if it were only that easy)! Especially in 2008 and beyond, communication and collaboration are now key factors. An article published by *Booz & Company* in 2007 profiles the character and disposition needed by a CEO today, now described as an *inclusive leader:*

> Welcome to the era of the inclusive chief executive officer...To succeed in this new era, CEOs are finding that they must embrace and reflect

> the concerns of board members, investors, and other constituencies, including employees and government. Those who ignore the new rules do so at their peril. Today's inclusive CEOs must be willing to engage in dialogue…[and] surround themselves with managers and advisors who complement their own capabilities.
> —(*The Era of the Inclusive Leader*, June 13, 2007)

Perhaps embracing these management values would have benefited Robert Nardelli, CEO of *Home Depot* from 2000 to 2006. Although he has the longest tenure of any of the CEOs on the previous table, Nardelli's poor and abrasive communication skills and unwillingness to listen to shareholder opinion ultimately lead to his demise. An article in *The New York Times* on June 23, 2009, reports that in one of his final board meetings at *Home Depot*, Nardelli "directed the company's board to skip the company's annual meeting and forbid shareholders from speaking for more than a minute, using large digital timers to enforce the rule."

On the other hand, because stakeholders felt the following CEOs cared for the organization and its mission, Andrew Grove (Intel), John Chambers (Cisco), and Paul Gavin (Motorola), collectively all from the same period, were perceived not only as industry icons, but also as "brands." Their fiscal performances were not any better than their fallen comrades, but their communication skills and leadership images, and their passion for their company, engendered loyalty. Motorola, for example, was ranked in the year 2000 by the Council of Institutional Investors as one of the ten worst companies in terms of shareholder returns.

On closer examination, it becomes clear that character is the lynchpin connecting the "visionary" CEO with the "inclusive" CEO and opening the portal to a new archetypal leadership, the Servant Leader. When we look closely at Washington's leadership of his company (the Continental Army), we get remarkable insights into how Washington exemplified this dual dimension of leadership and how he integrated them into a holistic new typology. The conditions under which he operated are especially instructive in that he was, in effect, dealing with corporate politics (interfacing with the Continental Congress) and was incredibly gifted in doing so. In addition, his managerial skills (he was also a master of hands-on issues of planning and execution) were tested under the most challenging of conditions—war.

We study leadership in wartime for insights because the qualities that all CEOs and senior executives must have to be effective leaders are magnified on the battlefield. These include believing in and articulating the vision, forging a winning strategy, motivating the "troops," leading by example, and making difficult decisions that can adversely impact not only the decision-maker but the very life of the organization itself.

The more one reads about Washington, the clearer it becomes the he was a CEO who not only dealt with the perennial issues of budgets, hiring and firing, and maintaining morale in his organization; but he also dealt with his moral responsibility to the organization. He applied this moral commitment as a compass for staying on course to achieve his political (business) objectives. That is, he had the moral vision with which he motivated his personnel and through which he clarified the company's mission, goals, and objectives.

His success can also be attributed to his uncanny ability to conceive a strategy and then apply the appropriate tactics *deliberately* and with *restraint*, while maintaining a consistent strategic perspective. However, in the first few years of the war, his company seriously lacked *organizational coherence*; it almost put him out of business! Only his moral leadership provided the mortar and then the structure, which offset and finally eliminated the chaos of an incoherent organization. He was ultimately successful—and this is critical—because *he was committed to service first and foremost.* Power was a means, always circumscribed by self-discipline and guided by "Right Reason," with which to achieve something greater than his own self-aggrandizement. This was the source of his moral leadership.

This last point will also be explored in our *Lessons in Leadership:* How does one's motive or the reasons one has chosen a leadership role impact his or her decisions—in style, in substance, and in resulting effectiveness? What soul searching should an aspiring or practicing CEO be doing before and during one's ascendance to a position of leadership? What spiritual journey must be taken to come to the truth that lies within each soul, and how does that guide us in making sound decisions? What is "Right Reason" and how does it work? And what, *By George!* did Washington do?

The Crucible of Character

Forging the Attributes of Leadership

> "When a man does all he can, Though it succeeds not well, Blame not him that did it."
> —(Rules of Civility and Decent Behavior, George Washington, 1758. Rule 44)

George Washington worked tirelessly to fine-tune his dispositions. He even wrote a book, *Rules of Civility and Decent Behavior*, a primer on self-development through practiced self-discipline. As part of his regimen, he made a point of addressing others meticulously, according to their rank, title, and position in both his letters and speech: this was part of his practice of "in writing or speaking, give to every Person his due Title According to his Degree and the Custom of the Place" (Rule 39). In the primer, he stressed not only those social graces that would make him acceptable to the Virginia planters but also virtues that any CEO needs to succeed. Some other examples include:

- "Be no flatterer" (Rule 17)
- "When a man does all he can though it Succeed not well, blame not him that did it." (Rule 44)
- "Be not hasty to believe flying reports to the disparagement of any." (Rule 50)
- "Labor to keep alive in your breast that little spark of celestial fire called conscience." (Rule 110)

The application of these rules would prove an effective management tool. In these aphorisms, we see that Washington truly understood the difference between *demanding* excellence and *expecting* perfection; and he applied this distinction in every assessment of his general staff and field officers and their conduct of the war. Consequently, although ambitious and capable of righteous rage at cowardice and neglect of duty, Washington truly practiced a code of self-discipline and respect for people, bolstered by his belief in their inherent goodness. These were, for him, moral precepts which guided him in the genesis and evolution of his civic religion.

Besides moral courage, every CEO needs physical and mental toughness. This translates not only into focus and stamina but also into presence and courage. Modern CEOs tend to be limited to graduate business schools and management development classes to learn their leadership skills, whereas Washington had the wilderness and wars where his principles were tested and his character forged. Add to this a lack of emphasis on ethics and ethical behavior in today's higher education, which leaves the modern CEO with little foundation for character building or internalizing the tenets of moral leadership.

Washington's development began prior to the Revolution when he served Virginia as surveyor, diplomat, and colonel, heading the Virginia Militia. In 1748, he made an unbelievable trek in totally uncharted wilderness, through the rugged Blue Ridge/Allegheny Mountains, with no more than deer and Indian trails to guide him. From 1754 to 1756, in two major battle campaigns in attempts to oust the French from Fort Duquesne (now Pittsburgh), Washington, who was both in command and a subordinate officer, displayed what was to become his hallmark. He was very tall, especially for his time (about six-feet-four-inches) with a serious demeanor and a ramrod posture. Many, including Jefferson, acknowledged him as "the finest horseman in Virginia." He could ride into a camp of stragglers and earn immediate attention and commensurate respect.

On one 1,000 mile trek during this period through the western wilderness to deliver the French an ultimatum at Fort Duquesne, he and his aids walked, waded, canoed, and rode in driving rain and ice storms, often sleeping on frozen terrain. During one of the battles with the French and their Indian allies, Washington led a charge, and he shot and killed the French commander at close range. Several years later, during a military campaign and rout of British General Edward Braddock, Washington had three horses shot from under him, four musket rounds tear through his coat, and his hat shot off. Barely recovering from a severe bout of dysentery that left him weak and debilitated and required him to ride on a pillow, Washington rode back and forth amongst volleys and war whoops in attempts to reorganize and rally British regulars who panicked when ambushed by an unseen enemy hidden by a primeval forest. He was the only officer to survive (over 60 percent of the regiment dead and wounded), and riding hundreds of miles, Washington led what was finally a somewhat orderly retreat.

This pattern of being in the thick of the battle and a prime target, given his size, prominence, and penchant for white horses, proved to add to his charisma and his effectiveness as a leader. *He risked what his troops risked*, asking no more from them than he would ask of himself. And they saw, remembered, and told others of this and of his courage and commitment. Washington led by example, a simple precept often forgotten by today's CEO. Also, as we shall later see, he understood the limitations of his experience and education, read studiously to learn what he did not know, and surrounded himself with those whose experience and knowledge supplemented his own. He listened to counsel and learned from his mistakes, and although he encouraged input from his officers and others, he took full responsibility for the outcome.

Upon his resignation in 1758 as Head of Virginias

Regiments, twenty-seven officers wrote him, asking him to remain. Here is an excerpt from one letter:

> The mutual Regard that has always subsisted between you and your Officers, have implanted so sensible an Affection in the Minds of us all, that we cannot be silent…Your Presence only will cause a steady Firmness and Vigor to actuate in every Breast, despising the greatest Dangers, and thinking light of Toils and Hardships, while lead on by the Man we know and Love.
> —(George Washington Papers at Library of Congress, 1741–1799: Series 4 General Correspondence. 1741–1799)

His response was a model of self-effacement and affection, but he chose to retire—for now. As a French Commander and others remarked repeatedly, in spite of his "stately bearing" and "mild gravity," he was able to win the love of most of those with whom he dealt. He mastered the art through selfless acts of courage, of making himself loved.

By contrast, Sunbeam's former CEO Al Dunlap comes to mind. "Chainsaw Al," as he was often called, once commented in an interview in response to his abrasive management style, "If they want a friend, let 'em buy a dog." Dunlap, who was hired in July 1996, was fired in June 1998.

> ### Washington's Leadership Wisdom
> - Demand excellence, not perfection
> - Lead by example
> - Master the art of making oneself loved and respected

George Washington Becomes CEO

Accepting the Challenge of Leadership

> "No pecuniary consideration could have tempted me to have accepted this arduous employment…"
>
> —(George Washington, Acceptance Speech 1775)

Although preceded by some differences of opinion, on June 16, 1775, the Board of Directors (Continental Congress) unanimously elected George Washington as CEO of the company called the Continental Army. In his acceptance speech and in subsequent letters to family and friends, he details the motives for accepting the position:

- Washington sincerely believed his talents and experience were insufficient: "I do not think of myself equal to the command I am honored with."

- He pledges, however, to "exert every power I possess in their service."

- And finally, he refuses any compensation but concluding his acceptance speech to the Board by stating: "...no pecuniary consideration could have tempted me to have accepted this arduous employment at the expense of my domestic ease and happiness...I do not wish to profit from it." Washington humbly requests only an expense account (not even stock options)!

Two days later, on June eighteenth, he writes to Martha: "a kind of destiny has thrown me upon this service, I shall hope that my undertaking is designed to answer some good purpose."

Through such correspondence, confirmed by subsequent actions, it becomes clear that Washington's understanding of leadership came from the perspective of service—*a clear sense of the leader as servant*. He had an overwhelming sense that his personal honor and reputation were at stake as he was called to serve a purpose greater than his self-interest: "The Common Good."

In a letter to a friend, Burwell Bassett, he remarks: "May God grant that in spite of 'Want of knowledge,' I serve the common good without injury to my reputation."

To overcome what he believes was his inexperience, he writes of three virtues all successful leaders and CEOs must have:

- "A firm belief in our purpose"
- "Close attention to its execution"
- "The strictest integrity"

In Washington's view, these are necessary to fill any voids a CEO may have in *ability* and *experience*. But the animating energy comes from a deeper source—the sense of service and caring. Much of Washington's dynamic here is reflected in Robert Greenleaf's *The Servant as Leader*, published in 1970. In this essay, Greenleaf explains servant leadership:

> The servant-leader *is* servant first... It begins with the natural feeling that one wants to serve, to serve *first*. Then conscious choice brings one to aspire to lead. That person is sharply different from one who is *leader* first, perhaps because of the need to assuage an unusual power drive or to acquire material possessions...

Servant leadership does not imply the absence of ego but describes those who place the purpose of their service ahead of personal gain. Yet there is a yin and yang here, for they are also strongly driven to preserve their reputations, and this, joined by right reason, serves as an internal moral compass steering their actions toward true north. What is the basis for this type of leadership? Let us explore this.

Washington's personal education and public life provided him with exposure to what is often called "Republican Virtue." From both Cicero and Seneca, whom he read, and political discourse on republican government, which he experienced in politics and learned exchanges with his Virginia compatriots, Washington embraced the notion that human beings are endowed with a natural inclination to know the good and distinguish between right and wrong. Right Reason (the substance of what is right) comes from the social and political values in which one is schooled; the nature of one's obligations to one's community and society, for example, which one learns from one's particular social milieu and political culture including his secular schooling and his church attendance.

He was reared on these values, internalized them, and combined them with the classical values of ethics and public service clearly understood and widely shared by his contemporaries. Washington's character reflects what Jim Collins has identified as the pinnacle of leadership—Level Five. Level Five leaders combine personal humility with professional will. The first creates the commitment to serve, the second, the commitment to lead. This follows Greenleaf's description of servant leadership quoted earlier.

In a letter to Martha upon receiving his commission from Congress as General of the Continental Army, Washington outlines this:

> It has been determined that the…whole army raised for the defense of the American Cause shall be *put under my care* (italics added), and that

it is necessary for me to proceed immediately to Boston to *take Command of it* (italics added).
—(*Letters of Delegates to Congress*, George Washington to his wife, June 18, 1775)

This statement describes the extraordinary uniqueness of Washington's concept of leadership. Washington is the *care commander*; he is a caretaker of the cause, the mission for which his Board of Directors (the Continental Congress) gave him the position. He has authority and the power to command, and yet even when he is given broader powers (dictatorial powers during the crisis of 1777–1778), he never loses sight of his mission—his *calling to service*. He continues to sign his letters "Your Faithful and Obedient Servant" in every correspondence to Congress.

At the end of the war, when he could have been king, he rode to Annapolis where Congress presided, and with Thomas Jefferson's direction, Washington publicly orchestrated the resignation of his own military commission, rank, and powers. He was conscious of every detail and understood that he was setting precedent through each and every act and gesture. He was clear as to his motives and mission—serving to build a great institution—that would survive his tenure and determine the destiny of a nation.

We are reminded of what one observer has said about J.P. Morgan—who, in spite of his reputation for ruthlessness, created leaders and a lasting organization. One observer said of J.P. Morgan: "(his) power was important to his achievement, but what made the result exceptional was that he cared—*he cared for the quality of the institution.*"

The definition of great leadership is caring enough that although having power, one initiates the means where power is used to serve and not to hurt, a mantra of servant leadership. J.P. Morgan understood this power and was conscious that he, like Washington, was working to build an institution greater than himself.

Upon his resignation, Washington submitted his expense account to Congress, in which he detailed, by category and amount, every expense incurred over the eight years of the war. Washington had spent $160,074 of his personal monies—a huge sum in those times. Upon review of the expenses, Congress noticed the general made an error in his accounting: he shortchanged himself by about eighty-nine cents! This mistake was promptly rectified by Congress.

There are current examples of Washington's refusal to take a salary: Steve Jobs takes a dollar a year salary to return to Apple; Allan Questrom takes no salary but a percent of profit to take to the helm as CEO of Barney's. And consider the counterparts, like failed Merrill Lynch CEO, John Thain, who was ousted from the firm in the early part of 2009. Days before the failing brokerage firm was scheduled to be acquired by Bank of America Corporation, Thain suggested to the board that he should receive a $10 million bonus for dubious service! Under extreme pressure from the board and immense public disgust, considering the economic conditions, Thain then decided that it was not appropriate to request a bonus and dropped his request. This, however, did not stop numerous other Merrill Lynch executives who were all too ready to accept bonuses in the millions of dollars. The payout of these bonuses under Thain's direction has been harshly criticized. The firm reported disastrous earnings results: the investment bank lost $27 billion for the year, $15.31 billion of which was in the fourth quarter alone!

Why then were neither Jobs nor Questrom initially successful, and why, among other things, was

Thain shown the door? Perhaps this is a result of their motives for leading: driven by *ego* rather than *service*. Compare the leaders above to Roger Enrico, CEO of *PepsiCo*. Enrico gave up a year's salary ($900,000) to fund college scholarships for the children of *PepsiCo* employees, and the corresponding results were dramatic! Following his donation, *PepsiCo* returned record earnings and profits for four consecutive quarters. Years later, *PepsiCo* continues to thrive, even in an unpredictable market. In their 2008 letter to shareholders, *PepsiCo* announced yet another year of strong growth: net revenue grew 10 percent, core division operating profit grew 6 percent, and core return on invested capital was 29 percent.

Washington's Leadership Wisdom

- Character and commitment are better predictors of success than experience or education
- Be a moral leader. Lead from the high ground.
- In serving others, you serve your better self.

Communicating the Mission Statement

Making the Mission Statement Matter

> "These are the times that try men's souls, the summer soldier and the sunshine patriot will in this crisis, shrink from the service of his country."
> —(The Crisis, by Thomas Paine, December 23, 1776)

In surveying why CEOs fail, one of the most prevailing patterns is the inability or unwillingness to communicate. This occurs on two levels: internally to and with his/her personnel and managers and externally to the Board of Directors and other stakeholders.

Communication, at its most inspirational level, takes

the form of a Mission Statement. The Mission Statement is a clear, uplifting, energizing vision that translates into a strategy or guideline for action. Washington clearly and consistently articulated his mission statement through over one thousand memos and letters to the board, his officers, and other stakeholders whose "fortune" were dependent on the "company's" success. With Washington, every step was carefully thought through and often orchestrated. For example:

- His speech and correspondence in acceptance of his command stresses Servant Leadership.

- His understanding with Thomas Paine that the "company's" democratic principles were that ordinary people can be empowered to be freer, wiser, and more autonomous yet make good decisions in light of the organization's purpose (again, a Servant Leadership principle).

- To maximize the mission, he enrolled each individual in the vision by incorporating it in the General Orders of the Day, read each morning to the assembled troops.

- When confronted with crises, he called upon this vision to unify, uplift, and inspire.

By George!

In Thomas Paine's *Common Sense*, which sold over 120,000 copies (comparable to selling over one million copies today), we find the essence of the vision of leadership as the act of empowering each person in the organization: "We have it in our power to begin the world over again. A situation, similar to the present, hath not happened since the days of Noah until now. The birthday of a new world is at hand."

This became the driving force and the mission of this company. Washington understood that hierarchical leadership in terms of excessive bureaucracy and inherited position is unnatural, and that ordinary people can lead if allowed to lead themselves.

In *The Crisis*, we have Paine's continuation of this theme and an extension of the mission and its vision. Here, the use of the Mission Statement in the darkest hours comes at Valley Forge. Although Washington didn't write it, he owned it. He recognized the power of Paine's words and ordered it to be read by every line officer to their men each day. To ensure their commitment to this, Washington made this part of the General Orders of the Day. As Commander-in-Chief, he had to sign off on these orders every day. It sent a clear message of his commitment to the company's mission and of how leadership can *literally* rally the troops, especially during difficult times. From these inspired words, enlistments increased, desertions decreased, and the Continental Army was saved from extinction. The essay was again read to his more than five thousand troops during the crossing of the Delaware River, culminating the first great American victory at Trenton on Christmas Day.

Washington's communication skills went beyond his field communiqués. When communicating to Congress (his Board of Directors), Washington always under-promised and over-delivered. When he lost a battle, he did three things:

- He told the truth—his memos were models of transparency.
- He provided an explanation (*not* an excuse but an analysis).
- He supported his explanation with the facts.

Written almost immediately after being defeated in battle, Washington sent a letter to John Hancock, President of the Continental Congress ("Chairman of the Board"). An excerpt of the letter is provided below and is a good prototypical Washington communication. Notice that Washington provides the reasons (not an *excuse* but an *analysis*) of why the battle was lost:

> Sir, I am sorry to inform you that in this day's engagement we have been obliged to leave the enemy masters of the field. Unfortunately the intelligence received of the enemy advancing up...was uncertain and contradictory...This prevented my making a disposition adequate to the force with which the enemy attacked us on our right; in consequence of which the troops first engaged were obliged to retire before they could be reinforced.
> —(Correspondence from George Washington to John Hancock, September 11, 1777)

He concludes with battle losses and the like. Whenever possible, Washington quantified the outcome. *At no time* did the Continental Congress (Board of Directors) not know of his plans, the outcome, the strategy, and its reasons. He thereby achieved the three objectives that all CEOs must strive for:

- Paying due respect to the board by making them an *ongoing* partner in the business.
- Never surprising the board by withholding or failing to keep them in the loop on critical issues: i.e., those that could seriously impair the success of the company or put it out of business.
- Using *right reason*, he was clear as to his motives and moral responsibility and thus communicated not as a public relations ploy but because he saw them as true partners.

Compare this with some of our contemporary CEOs. It had been suggested that both Rich McGinn (former CEO of Lucent) and Durk Jager (former CEO of Proctor and Gamble) lost the confidence of their respective boards because they over-promised. That is, they were not only sunk by overly inflated earnings projections but by repeated shortfalls that their Executive Committees (certainly McGinn's) had advised them could not be met. In McGinn's case, it was reported that the weekend he was ousted, most board members had arrived planning to support him, even though this was after three consecutive missed forecasts. Without any prior notice or preparation, the board was presented with the fourth forecasting shortfall, and McGinn's fate was sealed.

The failure to communicate with the Board of Directors and other powerful opinion leaders (most often the former Chairman and CEO) can also precipitate one's downfall. Witness Michael R. Bonsignore, former CEO of *Honeywell*. Bonsignore's first error was keeping secret from the Board the details of a merger with *United Technologies* as reported in the *Wall Street Journal*: "Some directors were peeved, not because they didn't like the deal, but because they had to consider it under a compressed time schedule."

When Jack Welch of *GE* tendered a better offer, the board again complained. Not so much about the deal but of Mr. Bonsignore's seeming inability to navigate the integration process and the absence of sound communications. Again, quoting the *Wall Street Journal*: "Some directors felt they were learning more…from news reports than from Mr. Bonsignore."

Besides communication issues with the board, Bonsignore failed to develop an ongoing relationship with Larry Bossidy, former CEO of *Allied Signal*. Bossidy's tentacles deeply penetrated the offices of many senior executives and board members, and his lack of confidence in Bonsignore is well-documented. Bossidy ultimately helped engineer Bonsignore's downfall.

Compare this to Washington, who corresponded to request assistance and seek advice from numerous individuals, including lukewarm supporters. Even Jack Welch, when he was considering a major strategic change, invariably consulted his predecessor, Reginald H. Jones, although Welch was under no organizational obligation to do so.

Finally, the mission statement will be meaningless unless the CEO personally and publicly promotes its value propositions both in everyday tactical as well as strategic circumstances. Tactically, as noted earlier, the mission value propositions were used by Washington to inspire recruits to continue their service (stay with the company after their "employment" contracts had expired) at a time of dire need. Here is an excerpt from Washington's plea to his troops made at Valley Forge when many were about to go home:

> You have done all I asked you to do and more than can be reasonably expected. But your country is at stake, your wives, your houses and all that

> you hold dear. You have worn yourself out with fatigues and hardships, but we know not how to spare you. If you will consent to stay...you will render that service to the cause of liberty and to your country which you probably never can do under any other circumstance.

First a few veterans, then others stepped forward. At day's end, over 1,200 stayed on to fight once again at Washington's side.

Henry Schacht, CEO of *Lucent Technologies* (1995 to 1997 and again from 2000 to 2002) understood Washington's emphasis on the mission. During a telecommunication crisis earlier in the decade, Schacht was quoted as saying that his role is "to rally the troops" and "restore their faith." Again, quoting Schacht: "You've got to make sure people have hope and believe."

A more recent example of this would be A.G. Lafley, who served as CEO of *Proctor & Gamble* from 2002 to 2009. Driving past the mission that had been in effect..."to improve the everyday lives of the customers," Lafley, driven by a vision of innovation as the soul of *P&G*, and not just a strategy, extended this mission statement to read: "The Consumer is Boss!"

He drove this mantra home through town hall forums with all employees and clearly set the metrics based on this mission by which employees would enjoy promotions and the corporation sustainable growth.

In this period, revenues doubled and margins/profits increased accordingly.

Washington's Leadership Wisdom
- Own the Company Mission as an inspirational belief and an operational practice
- Articulate the company's message both inside and outside the company
- Connect with shareholders and stakeholders through sincere, right reason

Charisma and Paradigm Leadership

"It is a sorry day when Buckskin can dictate to
a British General…"
—(General Edward Braddock, 1755)

Great CEOs are most often remembered for spearheading paradigm changes. They do so by their vision, character, and charismatic presence. At some point, they literally are transformed into brands. The process takes shape gradually and becomes complete when the individual's and the organization's core values seem indistinguishable. For example: Jack Welch of *GE*, Tom Watson of *IBM*, Bill Gates of *Microsoft*, and Steve Jobs of *Apple*.

Therefore, we come to believe in the leadership of this "brand" in the same way as we do with product brands; we trust their quality, consistency, authenticity, and the hopes they promise to deliver to us. Washington's evolution into a brand provided the insulation that saved him from being fired by his Board of Directors. Here is why:

After the disastrous defeats in 1777 on Long Island and in New York, Washington's military judgment and leadership qualities were broadly questioned and seriously doubted. A meeting by Congress to consider his removal petered out. Why? John Adams, who was not a particularly strong supporter of Washington, put it this way: "No other man can lead us for no other man is so identified with our cause."

All great CEOs have charisma that is a pre-condition for evolving into the stature of a brand—that special quality enables an individual to influence or inspire others, often large numbers of people. Washington had it in spades. Charisma seems to be a combination of the following:

- A *powerful, physical presence* (not necessarily limited to size)

- An *inner core of strength* that visibly radiates outward
- *Extraordinary exploits* often bordering on the miraculous and always the stuff that legends and stories are made on (long hours, near failures, overcoming seemingly insurmountable obstacles, etc.)

Finally, the paradigm shifts led by the individual seem to succeed only when the charismatic leader, articulating his vision, is seen as a brand which certifies that *the mission is legitimate and the vision attainable.*

Let us look at how Washington developed in this regard and how he compared with contemporary CEOs. From 1755 to 1758, Washington served as an officer in the Virginia Militia on the Western frontier that is now Western Virginia, Western Maryland, and Pennsylvania. As a colonial, he was subject to the disdain of British officers. They were aristocrats who failed to see that they were soon to be victims of a paradigm change. America's terrain and the independent spirit of self-made men would transform European military practices. They would do so by rendering traditional formation, volley, and charge tactics less than effective, and artillery, given the terrain, often an albatross around their necks.

Consider again the Wilderness Campaign, where the British planned to capture Fort Duquesne (modern-day Pittsburgh) from the French, during the French and Indian War (1755–1759). An elite British Army commanded by General Braddock found itself deep in an uncharted wilderness. The long line of men, wagons, cannons, and cattle could be seen for miles as it snaked its way through the Appalachian backcountry. The French, knowing they were outnumbered and outgunned, came out of the fort, which Braddock, using classic European siege tactics, was planning to take. The French *changed* the strategic paradigm by behaving proactively, giving up the defense of their fort and embracing unconventional tactical warfare.

Hiding in the woods with their Native American allies, they began firing down on a dazed, baggage-burdened British Army trapped by narrow trails. Reloading between blood-curdling war whoops, the French and their allies ran from tree to tree, unseen save for puffs of musket fire, raining down musket shot upon a helpless, frightened, disarray of men. Military discipline dissolved; the British panicked, broke ranks, often firing aimlessly at an enemy they could not see. Soon they were inadvertently gunning down their own, as the enemy without and the enemy within became one.

Recognizing that European "business" models wouldn't work here, Washington tried in vain to advise General Braddock that classic formation tactics in battle would court disaster. The woods and rugged terrain would be used by Native Americans and the French to decimate the cream of the British Army. Arrogance was a key factor that led to Braddock's downfall, much like the arrogance that led to the downfall of John deButts of *AT&T* and so many modern "captains" of industry.

William McGowan, founder and CEO of *MCI*, approached deButts with an offer to negotiate the connections to its local phone network. According to FCC regulations, *AT&T* was required to provide local connections at reasonable prices. However, deButts, being the arrogant leader that he was, thought little of anyone or any company who would dare compete with *AT&T*'s vast network and iconic stature and was quoted as saying: "You know we eat guys like you every day of the week."

In the face of all of this arrogance, both Washington and McGowan envisioned a paradigm shift that would alter how military and commercial battles were to be waged and won. Flexibility, speed, and individual initiative were recommended over hierarchy, formal maneuvers, and organizational rigidity.

In the end, deButts lost his job, and *AT&T* an enormous business opportunity, and Braddock lost his life. Braddock's often quoted remark in rejecting Washington's advice, "It is a sorry day when Buckskin can dictate to a British General," points to his inability to see that he had entered a New World.

Washington's leadership developed, and his charismatic legend was accentuated in the western wilderness. With the slaughter of Braddock's army, all the British officers were also killed or wounded. Originally relegated to a subordinate position to Braddock and his officers, Washington took charge. He had the wounded Braddock removed from the battlefield. Washington had three horses shot out from under him and four musket balls pass through his coat and hat, yet he was not wounded. He rallied what was left of the troops and led an orderly retreat. This is the stuff from which legends and leadership are made.

Washington's Leadership Wisdom

- Risk and lead paradigm change—expect resistance from entrenched stakeholders
- Test the paradigm in a real situation before launching it
- Translate the paradigm into an operational business model

George Washington as CEO

Thinking Strategically, Acting Tactically

"…There are those…who think the cause is not to be advanced otherwise than by fighting."
—(George Washington: A Biography, by Washington Irving, 1859)

Like other legendary CEOs, Washington's legacy was his ability to effect a major paradigm change. The shift in paradigm thinking began from his experience in the western wilderness and matured during his command of the Continental Army. Here, his success was based on knowing his company's strengths and weaknesses. He understood, for example, that he could draw on the ordinary worker (soldier) to put in overtime or for his managers (field officers) to take pay cuts or fight without periods of pay. He also knew that because they were fighting for home and family, they would endure many more hardships than the British or the Hessians. He knew that he had time and a vast, undeveloped countryside as strategic allies. Add to this that the British wanted a quick end to the war so to bring their resources to bear in other global "markets." And, as we have seen, they were unaccustomed to fighting undercover but looked to large battles through classic open field formations, where lines of soldiers fired, loaded, and charged.

Washington knew his army was not capable of such an execution; he lost virtually every battle when he attempted these tactics. He knew his company's weaknesses and his manager's vulnerabilities and managed each accordingly.

Management guru and author, Peter Drucker, developed a fundamental concept that all CEOs need to consider when planning groundbreaking strategic moves. In considering the adoption of new strategic initiatives, Drucker advised that a CEO should first ask: "what failure could put the company out of

By George!

business?" Washington understood this, mimicking British strategy and field tactics, and confusing victories with "victory" would surely put the Continental Army "out of business." Here's why:

European paradigms of land war held that whichever army "occupied" or "held" the battlefield after the battle was the victor. Resisting this model and communicating clearly to his field generals, Washington refused to succumb to false pride and even faultier strategies. He committed to a Fabian Strategy, named after the famous Roman General who had the Carthagians pay such an exorbitant price for their "victories" that they depleted their resources both material and spiritual and lost the will to fight. Washington and his general staff were committed to this strategy. In the 1777 campaign and in the shadow of total defeat, they devised a plan that should they be defeated they would retreat to the backwoods of Virginia and Pennsylvania and carry on a guerrilla war with the remnants of the Continental Army.

Foregoing European paradigms about what constituted victory, Washington gave up any thought of trying to defend the cities (larger markets) including Philadelphia, the then Capital to Congress (his Board of Directors). In effect, Washington found niche markets he could call his own, such as Valley Forge, Morristown, and West Point.

His plan was always to keep the British and General Howe from his supply bases. So long as he had access to blankets, forage, food, and ammunitions, he could continue his war of attrition. So, tactically, he kept his army between the two. As long as he had access to loyal supporters (his customers) in Pennsylvania, Virginia, and New York, and dependable supply chains, he could fight on almost indefinitely. He therefore adhered to a principle rule of business, in the words of Jack Welch: "Never allow anyone to get between you and your customers or your suppliers. Those relationships take long to develop and are too valuable to lose" (*Jack—Straight From The Gut*, by Jack Welch, page 348).

Finally, he knew that the Army was synonymous with the country; to lose the Army would be to lose the Republic. So he saved it at all cost, for he never lost sight of his ultimate goal—*Freedom from the Crown*.

Washington's ability to choose field generals who understood his strategy is clearly shown in his choice of Nathaniel Greene to head the Southern Army after

General Gate's battlefield fiasco. Greene "loses" battle after battle but inflicts greater casualties on the British than his army suffered. In his report to Washington, he proudly recites the mantra of this strategy: "We fight, lose, and rise to fight again."

As with any good CEO, Washington consistently articulated a strategy based on his assessment of his resources and the strengths and weaknesses of his organization compared to the competition. Here is his positioning statement:

> On our Side the War should be defensive...we should on all Occasions avoid a general Action, or put anything to the Risque, unless compelled by a necessity...With these views, and being fully persuaded that it would be presumption to draw out our Young Troops into open ground, against their Superiors both in number and Discipline.
> —(From George Washington to Head Quarters, New York, September 8, 1776)

The resources needed to implement such a strategy are primarily:

- morale
- money for recruitment
- materials

Long on morale but short on money, Washington worried that the militia would remain undisciplined and undependable. Congress worried that a professional army recruited for three-year enlistments would be too costly to the Treasury and would threaten American liberties. Washington worried that with more money, the British would recruit American Loyalists faster than he could recruit American Patriots.

And everyone was right! Consequently, Washington's tactics were often dictated by impending enlistment endings and the militia's lack of discipline in the field, something that professional soldiers have as a matter of course.

The most famous example of this occurred when he crossed the Delaware River in December 1777. In an unparalleled tactical attack at Trenton, picking Christmas Day and attacking in a snowstorm, he caught the entire Hessian garrison by surprise. Why were these tactics so successful? Because in Europe, *these tactics were inconceivable*. No army fought on

By George!

Christmas or attacked in a snowstorm. Their conventional expectations had done the British in. Washington did the unexpected, *compelled by a necessity*, since many of his militia men were about to return to their farms and the remainder of the army's enlistments were to end on January second!

Washington continued to follow his strategic guidelines to a T. The victory at Trenton was followed just a few days later by another smashing tactical success at Princeton. Here, Washington once again defied traditional military logic. Washington's army was pinned in with the Assunpink River in front of his troops and the Delaware at his rear. This left Washington's army blocked from retreat and cut off from his supply lines. General Charles Cornwallis, with a much larger force, was positioned facing the Assunpink River, the Delaware River, and Pennsylvania. No professional army would have left a stronger force, such as Cornwallis's, between his army and the territory (New Jersey) they were supposedly to defend, thus tradition said, Washington would fight. The British laughed at his "blunder." So confident was Cornwallis that he and his eight thousand fresh British troops retired for dinner and waited until morning to attack. As a ruse,

Washington's troops left barn fires burning, and a few men dug defensive embankments as if to prepare for the inevitable battle with the British the following day. That same evening, Washington's entire army of over five thousand men, with rags wrapped around their artillery wagon wheels to blunt the sounds, disappeared into the night.

Cornwallis's boast, *"I'll bag the fox in the morning,"* went from confidence to calamity as Washington's army, with few supplies and little equipment, marched throughout the night, moving twice as fast as any professional army of its time; then attacked and defeated several British Regiments and its garrison at Princeton.

Cornwallis *underestimated his competition* by assuming Washington would behave as British strategy dictated. But in war, as in business, strategies change with circumstances—only objectives remain constant.

Here in this unfettered country, unhampered by tradition, free men made their own military rules. Knowing this was also a war in which public opinion was an asset to be wisely nurtured, Washington eclipsed six months of defeats with two dramatic blows and two sudden victories. Morale increased, enlistments were extended, and local and state militia suddenly responded more willingly to the call to arms; and Europe listened, particularly France, bringing hard currency and equipment to the American cause.

A crumbled piece of paper was retrieved from where Washington had been sitting prior to crossing the Delaware. It read, in his handwriting: "Victory or Death."

Content with his victories, he did not continue on from Princeton to New Brunswick, which was unguarded and with stores of money and munitions. He took his tired army to Morristown and bivouacked for the winter. In a letter to John Hancock, again he explains why: "The harassed state of our own troops (Many having had no rest for two nights and a day) and the danger of losing advantage we gained by aiming at too much…" This combination of boldness, a willingness to risk everything, with deliberativeness and restraint characterized Washington's leadership.

Washington's Leadership Wisdom

- Learn your company's strengths, weakness, and resources
- Determine which weaknesses can put you out of business
- To minimize weaknesses, apply deliberative tactics consistent with new paradigm strategies

Management by Trust

Building a Management Team

> "He has a Faculty of Concealing his own sentiments...(and) A Faculty of discovering the sentiments of others..."
> —(The French Ambassador, 1778)

Washington took command of a company devoid of middle and upper management. Therefore, much of the operational details fell upon him. Yet he knew that decisions had to be made collegially and they were, in councils of war ("Executive Committee" meetings). This was because when the war broke out, Washington had little tactical experience with artillery and supplies, had never fielded or commanded a force larger than a thousand men, and had never formulated a strategic plan. He was ill-prepared for the task of combating tens of thousands of foreign troops from the world's most dominant navy and most professional army. How did he proceed to make up for these deficiencies?

- He counted on the collective wisdom, through Councils of War, of practical men who comprised his General Staff.
- He chose both friends and family members as advisors and field commanders.

The reason for this latter approach was not "the old boy network" or nepotism but something more substantial—loyalty. In the absence of experience, those *who put the cause above their own ambition* and tied their wagon to Washington's star were simply more dependable and predictable than the field generals who clearly saw the war as a chance to win not liberty but fame and fortune. Washington knew he sometimes needed the brilliant leadership of a General Charles Lee or a General Benedict Arnold, but he also knew that the cause for these men was merely an opportunity for self-aggrandizement. He understood that rather than having skill sets such as strategic planning and tactical brilliance, a new company needed first and foremost a committed, loyal, and disciplined young officer staff (his corporate managers). These staff members had to embrace discipline, loyalty, and commitment and, setting aside personal objectives, focus on the company's mission.

These management perspectives can be seen operating in today's business world. Soon after joining *Sunbeam* as CEO in 1998, Jerry Levin began recruiting senior managers from his former employer, *The Coleman Company*, this necessitated by the need to jump-start the process of fixing *Sunbeam's* appalling record in operations and execution. In Levin's words: "I had to bring in people who knew me. They would have the confidence that I could hold this thing together. It looked so bad, how could you recruit (elsewhere)?"

The same loyalty and commitment to the company and its mission is the hallmark of Henry Schacht's vision as interim CEO at *Lucent*. Chosen to put *Lucent* back on course, one of his first objectives was: "To reassure his troops and restore their faith that the problems ... can be fixed."

In May 2001, when *Lucent's* CFO, Deborah

Hopkins, seemed more concerned with her career than with *Lucent's* revival, she was asked to leave. Schacht, it was reported, was looking for loyal and committed employees who would help restore *Lucent* to its former glory. Differing with him on strategies for *Lucent* and given Hopkins's incessant focus on her desire to become CEO (as well as her openly voiced concerns as to how *Lucent's* problems would impact her reputation), made Schacht's decision relatively easy.

Washington faced similar situations to Schacht's. The General had exceptional instincts for assessing men's character and reading their motives. Though cold and calculated in his dealings with subordinates, he could win their love (loyalty). Those whose loyalties were questionable or clearly without real commitment would eventually lose their positions in the company. It is indicative that the three most experienced generals, Charles Lee, Benedict Arnold, and Horatio Gates, were all, at the war's end, disgraced and without commands for acts ranging from gross and repeated ineptness to treason.

Take Gates, for example. Establishing his reputation by defeating and affecting the surrender of the British and General John Burgoyne at Saratoga in October 1777, Gates grew heady. However, Washington knew that the victory was not the result of Gates's leadership ability; rather, it was the result of Burgoyne's troops being vastly outnumbered and his supply lines stretched beyond logistical effectiveness. Although Washington was his superior, Gates purposely did not inform him of the victory; he communicated directly with Congress. Gates then lobbied Congress for Washington's position and was involved in several intrigues to effect his removal. Washington remained cool and in a letter to Gates counterattacked with dignity, which resulted in an apology from Gates. Washington did not publicly counter Gates before Congress, for that would have placed Gates, literally and figuratively, on an equal plane with Washington. The General understood the relationship between power, perception, and leadership.

Though he enjoyed victory at Saratoga, Gates had refused to follow the Councils of War, which could have cost him the battle! A few years later, in his arrogance, he repeated the same mistake at Camden, South Carolina, in the Southern Campaign. In spite of the overwhelming recommendation of his general staff, Gates refused to do a troop count and grossly miscalculated the number of troops under his command. His attack strategy was based on twice his actual troop strength. It was a disaster, and he fled the battlefield and rode to a safe haven in shame without attempting to rally his broken troops.

Washington immediately replaced him with Nathaniel Greene, an officer with a mixed field record. In 1776, Greene was the one who had strongly advised Washington to hold and defend a hopeless Fort Washington, almost resulting in the end of the war and victory for the British. But again, Washington was extremely adept at knowing the limitations and the strengths of his generals. He gave field regiments and field commanders a chance to redeem themselves even after cowardice or incompetent action or leadership. This was one of Washington's patient strengths. Invariably, those who failed him and the cause the first time, when given another chance, proved him a shrewd motivator of men. He understood the difference between expecting perfection from his men and striving for excellence.

His choice of Greene was based on Greene's total commitment to Washington and his guerilla strategy. Short on supplies, mobile in their tactics, and living off the land, Greene's talent aligned perfectly with the task. He was an outstanding Quartermaster who knew how to locate, requisition, and distribute supplies in what seemed like an endless stream—prerequisites for keeping his army in the field and harassing the British until his Continentals could attack with superior numbers.

On the other hand, there was Benedict Arnold, who was possibly the most able general of the war. He was, however, filled with arrogance and personal ambition, and Washington knew this. He had married a woman rich and much younger than he and soon found himself part of a lavish and expensive lifestyle. As military head administering Philadelphia, Arnold came under suspicion for misuse of public funds and other questionable administrative practices.

Innuendos abounded, yet Washington did not go to his defense, nor did he give him the position of a field command, in spite of Arnold's continued requests and Washington's belief that Arnold, from a purely military perspective, deserved it. Why? Because Washington correctly read and distrusted Arnold's motives, though Washington never imagined that Arnold would take it as far as he did. Congress also refused Arnold's requests, and the rest is history.

Feeling underpaid and under-appreciated, he went over to the competition. But Washington again knew Arnold's brilliance was overshadowed by his self-serving ambition, so, again, he refused to alter his philosophy that loyalty, given the nature of the war, was a superior virtue to that of talent.

Washington's unyielding commitment to this management model went so far as to include Lafayette, whom he truly loved as a son. Lafayette, the aristocrat and French citizen, had come from France to serve in the cause and had proved to be an effective field officer. Suspecting that his unbridled enthusiasm to lead a Canadian Campaign to capture Montreal could lead to French ascendancy in Canada (which might have been encouraged by Lafayette), Washington diplomatically refused to grant Lafayette's request for a field commission (he later does appoint him to one at Yorktown when victory appeared imminent and a Canadian strategy was no longer in play).

Finally, there was General Charles Lee, the only "senior executive" who had a formal military education and military field experience. He had come to America from England in the 1760s to seek his fortune. Imperious, arrogant, and idiosyncratic, he thought himself superior in every way to Washington, whom he considered to be a military bungler. Washington was, nonetheless, always extremely deferential to him, even after discovering that Lee made remarks critical of Washington's leadership. Nevertheless, Washington gave him a command at the crucial Battle of Monmouth. The cause was more important than Washington's personal feelings.

The extent of his arrogance can be seen in his arrangement with Congress. He accepted his commission as a general, second in command to Washington, only if he were reimbursed should any of his property be confiscated by the British for his joining up with the rebels.

Lee's first insubordination occurred in 1777 when Washington's army was shattered in retreat, pursued by the British across New Jersey, where it appeared that its surrender was imminent. Lee, seeing a chance to win Washington's command, purposely misinterprets Washington's *order* to bring Lee's army to his aid as a *suggestion*. At Monmouth, a year later, Lee gets the field command because his rank as the senior officer entitled him to it. Yet again, he countermands Washington's order—this time to attack. The Americans had the British surrounded and could possibly have dealt them a fatal blow, but Lee failed to act. Only Washington's personal appearance on the battlefield rallying the troops saved the day. After that, Washington immediately had Lee arrested and court marshaled.

> ### Washington's Leadership Wisdom
> - Loyalty can be a temporary substitute for lack of experience
> - Be clear about your personal agenda so you can read the motives of others
> - Reward loyalty openly and deal with disloyalty quickly and openly

Operations and Delegations

Managing the Details of New Strategies

> "War must be carried on systematically, and to do it, you must have good officers…"
> —(George Washington, 1776)

Micromanagement may have been given a bad rap. Its function or dysfunction really depends on circumstances. For example, whether introducing a new strategy, repositioning an existing division, or launching a new product, a CEO should be, in these instances, hands-on. Articulating the vision and igniting the passions of management may not be enough. At the outset, successful CEOs are both visionaries *and* micromanagement motivators. They never confuse delegation with abdication and realize "the devil is in the details." Therefore, the leader must make this commitment clear through his/her own *specific guidelines*.

Given the conditions under which he operated, Washington was a micromanager. Washington was notorious in his penchant for detail, for he had two serious organizational shortcomings to address:

- His lack of trained officers (field or operations managers). During the battles for New York City, a field officer, Major General Henry Knox, wrote: "The General is as worthy a man as breathes, but he cannot do everything and be everywhere. He wants (needs) good assistants. There is a radical evil in our Army—The lack of officers."

- His troops were not professional soldiers. Militia men were loyal to their States (departments) and were accustomed to coming and going as they pleased. (A culture where employees felt entitlements.)

By George!

He approached these shortcomings in the following ways:

- He established his source of authority over disorderly troops he inherited by ordering his commanding officer to read aloud his commission to his troops. He prominently showed himself during these communications.

- He announced a new command structure and detailed operational order. These he wrote and read aloud—including materials, costs, and timelines…everything down to the size of certain equipment.

- He ordered that specific infractions draw specific penalties. These were promulgated in detail.

- He specified that all matters of procedure and discipline included the times when certain operations should take place.

- He delivered rewards conspicuously and personally and made sure punishments were made public.

As we shall see, Washington's sense of discipline, detail, and focus were similar to Jack Welch's (CEO of GE). Only at times, Washington had to micromanage because he created an infrastructure from scratch and conducted the war most often without experienced middle managers.

Washington changed America's army into a professional, highly motivated mobile organization. This is similar to Jack Welch when he came and shook up the established culture of polite engineers that thought him aggressive and pushy—and hell-bent on changing every aspect of *GE*.

It began with "the boundary-less" corporation, which eschewed bureaucracy and hierarchy and culminated with Six Sigma, which instilled a fierce morale and commitment to excellence in the ranks. Washington and Welch had much in common. For example, Jack Welch is often quoted as saying: "I don't run *GE*—I lead *GE*."

Yet when he led GE toward its new, unprecedented commitment to implement and realize Six Sigma quality control standards within five years (it had taken Motorola ten years!), he understood the necessity of the following:

By George!

- He discussed it in every speech he gave.
- He followed with a pamphlet about how and why it was essential to the future of *GE* and every employee.
- At the *GE* Operating Managers Meeting, he tied the commitment to Six Sigma to "getting on board"—or getting another job! Again, in his presentation he indicated how pervasive this commitment must be by specifying each arena of work activity (specifically meetings, speeches, reviews, promotions, and hiring) where the central message and the final objective must be Six Sigma.

Finally, to underline and personalize his commitment even further, he faxed managers around the world, detailing promotions requirements associated with the Six Sigma strategy, even stating dates when certain stages of training and passing of Six Sigma qualifying test must be passed as the price for retaining one's job!

Welch had the benefit of having in his ranks "many good officers (managers)" who could "systematically" make it happen. The result, *GE* from the inception of Six Sigma in 1996 has realized record growth and profits. Contrast this with the struggles of Carl Yankowski, CEO of *Palm, Inc.* (2000–2001). Yankowski attempted to institute a new strategy of positioning *Palm* as a provider of wireless hand-held solutions instead of just a device-maker. The inclusion of software would put *Palm* well ahead of *Microsoft's Merlin* and keep it the industry leader.

When he met with his production and operations managers, he asked if the new *Palm m500* and *m505* could be manufactured and brought to market before a certain timeframe. His operations team unanimously said "yes," without instituting a detailed system of monitoring or assessing this promise. Not realizing the lack of managerial sophistication of his team, Yankowski prematurely announced the launch of the new models. Customers held off on their purchases to wait for the new models, leaving existing *Palm* inventory on the shelves gathering dust. The new models arrived two months after the announcement, though they were supposed to be ready in two weeks, resulting in an inventory write-off loss of $300 million, lay-offs of 300 employees (almost 18 percent of their work force), and fall-off in market valuation of over 70 percent.

In light of this, Yankowski began to attend *Palm's*

operations council meetings and hired several experienced operations managers. However, his failure to focus on and provide detailed guidelines for the new product launch cost him and the company dearly. In his own words, "I was externally focused before and now I'm internally focused. We know we need to improve our Management talent and processes."

Shortly after this blunder, and after just two years as CEO, Yankowski resigned, citing a narrowing of his responsibilities by the board.

So what could Yankowski have learned from Washington? Washington consistently under-promised and over-delivered his duties. Washington organized, led, and motivated his "company." Biographer Robert J. Allison, author of *First in the Hearts of His Countrymen*, calls Washington the "First Modern American Corporate Executive." It is this "modernity" that makes his actions useful as guidelines for today's executives. "The Americans won... because Washington and his corporate family had introduced a new age ... that the British failed to adapt to." Winning was no longer about great battlefield generals but now was about patience, creativity, logistics, and attention to detail.

- "He understood the importance of morale, terrain, and transport" (Read: motivation, market conditions, and operations/logistics)
- "He was a master of improvisation, of trial and error"

Once clear about what worked, Washington, like Welch, had the steady discipline to stay with it and the vision to inspire and motivate those who would help to bring it all to fruition. He also had the toughness of mind and willpower to see it to a successful conclusion. But until it all coalesced, or when he feared it was coming apart, he micromanaged. One is reminded of CEO Mickey Drexler's observation after *GAP* reported its largest same-store sales decline in three years since September 2001: "We're getting back to the fundamentals that built this business. Those might mean micromanagement in some cases…Acting a bit more dictatorial…we're taking it back…I am spending my time at a much more intense level."

And during a period when its stock prices were falling and profits sinking, down 68 percent in the third quarter ending October 2001, then CEO Michael Eisner of *The Walt Disney Company* was back "in the trenches" micromanaging scripts! As reported, his approach was to challenge racy, crude language and circumstances with "old school values." Put simply, he was focused on returning *Disney* scripts to the promise of the *Disney* mission—and hopefully, to past patterns of profitability.

Returning for a moment to A.G. Lafley's mission to transform *P & G* into a truly consumer-centric culture driven by innovation: he too required adherence to detailed steps in both product development and risk management, which his team could use as metrics to determine their progress in this new milieu. To some, this included setting standards that seemed contrary to the interest of the corporation, e.g., that at least 50 percent of new products and methods should emanate from outside the company, especially from consumers. In 2001, 15 percent of new products came to *P&G* in this manner; by the end of 2008, new product innovation from ideas generated from the outside reached and exceeded the 50 percent target! In his words, "People became more willing to subjugate their egos to the greater good...Improving Consumer's Lives" (*The Game Changer* Ram Charan and A.G. Lafley, 2008).

Washington's Leadership Wisdom

- Micromanaging may be essential for start-ups, launches, or failing strategies
- Middle managers do not make strategies—they make strategies take hold
- CEOs should, without reservation, step into faltering field operations

Leadership by Example and Crisis Management

Leading by Example

> "Our affairs, according to my judgment are now come to a crisis and require no small degree of political skill, to steer clear of those shelves and rocks...which may wreck our hopes and throw us on some inhospitable shore."
> —(George Washington, 1779)

In August 1777, New Yorkers and the Continental Army awoke to what appeared to be a forest of masts bobbing in an open sea in New York Harbor. A massive British fleet had suddenly arrived with over one hundred warships and eighty troop transports, the largest armada ever assembled by the British. Anticipating an attack on Brooklyn but unsure if this was not an enemy ploy to distract the Americans from an offensive on New York City, Washington ferried almost half his army across the East River, where they took up positions waiting for the landing of British Red Coats on the beaches of Brooklyn.

That evening, ten thousand British and Hessian troops managed to come ashore undetected. They got behind the American lines and left flanks and at dawn, surprised, routed, and almost eliminated this small army. Only Washington's appearance on the battlefield in the final moments brought order. He is described as follows: "Outwardly calm, imperturbable, and confident: whatever doubts may have gnawed at him."

He then, in the darkness of this foggy evening, decided that the position was indefensible. He ordered a retreat across the East River to Manhattan, in what became a blinding rainstorm. The orderliness and stealth under Washington's watchful eye would become a hallmark of his genius for logistics and leadership. An entire army, all of its equipment and supplies were ferried across a river without the enemy being aware. Had the British discovered the retreat and attacked, panic and the annihilation of his army was almost certain. Of this classic execution in logistics and leadership, a British military analyst writing at that time observed:

> Those who are best acquainted with the difficulty, embarrassment, noise, and tumult which attend even by day, with no enemy at hand a (troop) movement of this nature...will be the first to acknowledge that this retreat should hold a high place among military transactions.
> —(*The American Revolution*, Bruce Lancaster, 2001, page 149)

As one of the last boats pulled away, seen still on the Brooklyn beach stood "a very tall man, cloaked and booted coming down slippery steps to an outstretched hand." Washington was the last to leave. This scene was to repeat itself time and time again.

Washington on the front line, Washington the last to leave an evacuation, retreat, or a staged attack; Washington always led by example. Save for some special dispensation, it is difficult to understand how he repeatedly survived such ordeals.

This was repeated again at the battle of Princeton.

Washington, riding on a huge white horse into the middle of the battlefield, rallied his failing troops to victory. An aide rubbed his eyes, sure that no man could emerge alive from the bullets and batteries. But when he looked up, there was Washington. Several months later at the battle of Monmouth, Washington entered the field, again on a large, easily seen white horse, and once again rallied his troops with his courage, coolness, and example. Here, Lafayette described him as he stopped the retreat to help ensure victory: "His presence stopped the retreat...his calm courage...gave him the air best calculated to excite enthusiasm...(he) rode all along the lines amid the shouts of the soldiers cheering them by his voice and example and restoring to our standards the fortune of the fight..." In no way do we find Washington's leadership and steely determination more apparent than in the ultimate crisis: the treason of Benedict Arnold.

In 1780, Arnold had been made commandant of West Point. At that time, it was the vital strategic outpost defending not only the Hudson Valley but approaches to New England as well. Bitter over not being fully exonerated during a Court Martial and never given the recognition due to him and full rank and general's pay, Arnold maneuvered Washington for this post in preparation for selling out both the Fort and Washington for twenty thousand British pounds. Washington discovered the plot and remarked to his aids: "Arnold has betrayed us; who can I trust now?"

What was now the most serious crisis of the Revolution required crisis management of the highest magnitude. Firstly, he remained remarkably calm, showing no outward signs of the turmoil within. Then he moved accordingly:

- He shifted the command of regiments that had fought under Arnold to other officers.
- He put his most trustworthy general, Nathanial Greene, in charge of West Point.
- He brought his best and most seasoned troops to West Point.
- He ordered the trial and execution of Arnold's British accomplice John Andre (Arnold having escaped) and carried out the sentence swiftly. Andre was hung in public.
- He launched a secret plot to have Arnold, who was now a British General, assassinated.
- He immediately issued statements to the

nation to the effect that only those in Arnold's family and Andre were in on the plot, ensuring national cohesion.

- He personally and conspicuously took control of the crisis and its management.

The effect of this, especially the latter, was to restore confidence and calm and to avoid witch hunts that would have undermined the cohesion of the army and the nation. In his words: "By sowing jealousies, and if we swallow the bait no [one's] character will be safe. There will be nothing but mutual distrust."

Finally, Washington made what could have lingered as a loss of faith in the cause into a positive, almost prophetic vision vis-à-vis the outcome, by issuing this statement to Congress, the army, and the American people: "In no instance since the commencement of the war has the interposition of Providence been more conspicuous than in the rescue of the post and garrison of West Point from Arnold's villainous perfidy."

His final act of leadership by example and crisis management came during the Newburgh Conspiracy of 1783. Congress had continuously failed to live up to its promised payments to officers and men. The

By George!

military, his field-line officers, were plotting to take over the government. Washington was invited to join them or to step aside. All of the objectives for which the cause and campaigns had been waged were suddenly in danger of being lost, including the very life of the organization itself. He approached this crisis as he did all others: calmly and always giving the benefit of the doubt to his men. His statement during the mutiny of a New Jersey regiment several years earlier reflects this: "They cannot be in earnest, they have only reasoned wrong about obtaining a good end."

Washington countered by calling a meeting but hinting that he would not personally attend. He took the officers, all of whom had fought with him, off guard when he showed up and strode onto a small platform. At first, his speech, which called for moderation and trust in the government's eventual fairness, seemed ineffective. Here is the concluding portion:

> Let me entreat you...not to take any measures...which will lessen the dignity and sully the glory...you have maintained. You will, by the dignity of your conduct afford prosperity to say—Had this day been wanting, the world

had never seen the last stage of perfection to which human nature is capable of attaining.
—(George Washington, March 17, 1783)

The officers did not react. They were seemingly unmoved by his plea for patience. Up to that time, he had been speaking without notes, but he had a brief letter from the Congress, which he then pulled from his coat pocket, hoping to read it and reassure the officers as to Congress's good intentions. But as he fumbled to open the single page, he seemed to become disoriented, unable to read the text. The officers in the hall stirred and became uneasy. Then Washington took his glasses from his inside coat pocket, which only his inner circle of officers had ever seen him wear, and remarked: "Gentlemen... you will permit me to put on spectacles, for I have not only grown gray but almost blind in the service of my country."

The battle-hardened soldiers wept almost en masse. The mutiny was over. Washington's simple statement, unprepared and from his honest heart, had done what no amount of logic or oratory reason could achieve. In Jefferson's words, "The moderation and virtue of a single character probably prevented this Revolution from being closed, as most others have been, by a subversion of that liberty it was intended to establish."

> ## Washington's Leadership Wisdom
> - A crisis is an opportunity for leadership from the heart
> - In crisis, a calm demeanor is a leadership dynamic
> - Swift, publicly performed actions confirm the viability of the company

Conclusion

A survey on Corporate Image and Reputation found that over 50 percent of top executives believe that the public perception of the CEO is tantamount to the perception of the company. There was even stronger support for the notion that "A positive Corporate image (was) a prerequisite for achieving their strategic business objectives" (*Wall Street Journal*, February 27, 2001).

Although this responsibility for image enhancement is an ongoing responsibility of the CEO, nowhere does it show its importance more than in crisis. Witness Washington in the previous chapter and recall his ability to manage a crisis. Successful CEOs display similar action patterns. Here are some classic examples of role model behavior and its opposite.

In 1982, Jim Burke, CEO of *Johnson & Johnson*,

was faced with the Tylenol bottle-tampering crisis; the ultimate test of leadership was upon him. He could have listened to his director of public relations and not appeared on television to face the American public. But after soliciting many options, as did Washington on his ongoing council of war, he opted for openness, candor, and availability. His television appearance calmed a frightened nation and restored public confidence in the product and the brand. In spite of his mistaken assessment, Burke did not fire the PR director. As with Washington, Burke encouraged differing points of view and then made his own decision, but he did not summarily punish subordinates for errors made in earnest.

Compare this with the *Exxon/Valdez* environmental disaster or the *Ford/Firestone* accidents and tragic deaths. In both instances, the CEOs were defensive or blamed others. For Ford, the inability to meet the issues head on with moral leadership cost the company untold billions and cost *Ford's* CEO, Jacques Nasser, his job.

As we have seen, contributing to a CEO's staying power is the ability to consult and communicate with stakeholders, such as car dealerships and unions, on strategic changes as well as crisis management. Nasser failed to do either successfully and was ousted.

What is so interesting is that Mr. Nasser's failed program to eliminate weak managers through a grading/rating system (two "Cs" and your gone) was bitterly resisted, but a similar though more sophisticated program by Jack Welch was implemented and continues to be used by *GE*. One major difference was that Welch brought the idea to his colleagues, who helped fine-tune it and own it. Nasser didn't do this.

In summarizing the essence of Washington's greatness as a leader, an article by Holman W. Jenkins, Jr. of the *Wall Street Journal* provided this insight in his editorial commentary on Jack Welch (October 25, 2000). Welch is, in Jenkins view:

> An unparalleled psychological leader. His presence enables others to do things they wouldn't have been able to do without him standing behind them to absorb the psychic risk… [Welch has] a unique gift for unflinchingly assessing the realities and fearlessly charging toward the opportunity.

This statement represents an excellent definition of moral courage and inspirational leadership. It could just as easily have been written to describe A.G. Lafley or … George Washington, CEO.

Post Script

I hope this book provides a point of departure for exploring the pressing question of leadership and CEOs: how do we re-tool our institutions to develop *character* in our leaders and its counterpart, *integrity*? What role does a sense of honor and love of duty play in fostering civic virtue in a culture where disparate diversity is honored more than common cause?

How do we bring the power of protecting one's personal reputation into line with serving the common good so each serves the tenets of the other? How do we identify right reason and bring its promise to bear on public life?

What we can learn from Washington's leadership principles is how the power of Service can be harnessed to drive both the public good and personal ambition... that leadership, when it is moral leadership strapped in by the tenets of "Right Reason," enables these seemingly contradictory objectives to become compatible. What has been, traditionally in Western thought, seen as irreconcilable and therefore unachievable, is within our grasp. We need only the courage to begin a paradigm shift and the faith to sustain it.

A Summary of Washington's Leadership Guidelines

The Attributes of Leadership

- Demand excellence, not perfection
- Lead by example
- Master the art of making oneself loved

The Challenges of Leadership

- Character and commitment are better predictors of success than experience or education
- Be a moral leader
- Serve others to serve your better self

Mission Statement as Leadership Mantra

- Own the *Company Mission* as an inspirational belief and an operational practice
- Articulate the company's message both *inside* and *outside* the company
- Connect with shareholders and stakeholders through sincere right reason

Leading With the Paradigm

- Risk and lead paradigm change—expect resistance from entrenched stakeholders
- Test the paradigm in a real situation before launching it
- Translate the paradigm into an operational business model

Leading the Strategy with Tactical Deliberation

- Learn your company's strengths, weaknesses, and resources
- Determine which weaknesses can put you out of business

- To minimize weaknesses, apply deliberate tactics consistent with new paradigm strategies

Building a Management Team

- Loyalty can be a temporary substitute for lack of experience
- Be clear about your personal agenda so you can read the motives of others
- Reward loyalty openly and deal with disloyalty quickly and openly

Systematic Managing

- Micromanaging may be essential for start-ups, launches, or failing strategies
- Middle managers do not make strategies—they make strategies *take hold*
- CEOs should, *without reservation*, step in to faltering field operations

Leading In Crisis

- A crisis is an opportunity for leadership from the heart

- In crisis, a calm demeanor is a leadership dynamic
- Swift, publicly performed actions confirm the viability of the company

e|LIVE

listen|imagine|view|experience

AUDIO BOOK DOWNLOAD INCLUDED WITH THIS BOOK!

In your hands you hold a complete digital entertainment package. Besides purchasing the paper version of this book, this book includes a free download of the audio version of this book. Simply use the code listed below when visiting our website. Once downloaded to your computer, you can listen to the book through your computer's speakers, burn it to an audio CD or save the file to your portable music device (such as Apple's popular iPod) and listen on the go!

How to get your free audio book digital download:

1. Visit www.tatepublishing.com and click on the e|LIVE logo on the home page.
2. Enter the following coupon code:
   5192-c944-87fb-c82e-3c07-9479-373b-7644
3. Download the audio book from your e|LIVE digital locker and begin enjoying your new digital entertainment package today!